SILVER RING THING
COVENANT

In signing this covenant before God Almighty, I

_____

agree to wear a silver ring as a sign of my pledge
to abstain from sexual behavior that is inconsistent
with Biblical standards. On my wedding day, I will present
my silver ring to my spouse, representing my faithful
commitment to the marriage covenant.

*"God wants you to be holy, so you should keep clear
of all sexual sin. Then each of you will control your body
and live in holiness and honor."*
1 Thessalonians 4:3-4

_____
STUDENT SIGNATURE   DATE

_____
ACCOUNTABILITY PARTNER SIGNATURE   DATE

Denny Pattyn
SILVER RING THING
FOUNDER AND PRESIDENT
denny@silverringthing.com
Hebrews 12: 1-3

next

LIVING OUT YOUR
COMMITMENT
TO WAIT

student book
denny pattyn

Scripture quotations marked (NLT) are taken from the Holy Bible, New Living Translation, copyright © 1996. Used by permission of Tyndale House Publishers, Inc., Wheaton, Illinois 60189. All rights reserved.

Scripture quotations marked (ESV) are taken from The Holy Bible, English Standard Version, copyright © 2001 by Crossway Bibles, a division of Good News Publishers. Used by permission. All rights reserved.

Scripture quotations marked (NAB) are taken from the NEW AMERICAN STANDARD BIBLE®, Copyright © 1960, 1962, 1963, 1968, 1971, 1972, 1973, 1975, 1977, 1995 by The Lockman Foundation. Used by permission.

Scripture quotations marked (NIV) are taken from New International Version, copyright © 1973, 1978, 1984. Used by permission of The Zondervan Corporation, Grand Rapids Michigan 49530, U.S.A. All rights reserved.

Scripture quotations marked (NKJV) are taken from the New King James Version. Copyright © 1982 by Thomas Nelson, Inc. Used by permission. All rights reserved.

ISBN: 0-9771-2482-7

Printed by LJC Communications and Publishing
Moon Township, PA 15108
dpattyn@silverringthing.com

N E X T

*"Living Out Your
Commitment to Wait"*

The Bible studies in this book have been developed as a follow-up resource for students who have attended an SRT Live Show, an SRT *Get It On* Film Event or any other abstinence program. These studies are designed to be used in large or small groups lead by a youth leader. They are also an excellent resource for accountability partners or can be useful for individual study.

Take advantage of these special Bible studies. They are what you need to guide you through a youth culture that knows no boundaries. Remember, you are not alone; hundreds of thousands of teenagers just like you are "waiting." You can do this…With God's Help!

A decision of this magnitude will certainly require **"Supernatural Help."** You will need the Holy Spirit's presence speaking to you from within on a daily basis. These studies and devotions will challenge you to trust God more as you get to know Him better by spending time in prayer and in His word.

If you don't have a youth leader or parent to organize a group session to go through these Bible studies, please find an accountability partner or good friend who will agree to work through these 4-sessions with you. Start today!

> **"The Key Ingredient in living out an abstinence commitment is dynamic faith"** - *Denny Pattyn*

DEALING WITH TEMPTATION

LEARN

Ok, so you just made a commitment to abstinence…and you are now excited to live out your commitment in the real world. But, make no mistake, you are about to be chased down by enemy #1…TEMPTATION! No one gets through life without facing many forms of temptation, not even Jesus.

What's the point?

Temptation itself is not a sin, but falling into it is. After all, Jesus himself was tempted, yet he never sinned. So, if you don't want to fall into temptation, you will need to learn how to quickly **recognize** when you are being tempted and **avoid** situations that will lead you down the wrong road. When you do find yourself in a tempting situation, you will need to learn to **minimize** its effects by depending upon God's power and not your own strength. In doing so, you will not allow temptation to establish a foothold in your life.

REFLECT

Key Scripture - "He will provide a way out"

1 Corinthians 10:13 NIV [13]*No temptation has seized you except what is common to man. And God is faithful; he will not let you be tempted beyond what you can bear. But when you are tempted, he will also provide a way out so that you can stand up under it.*

James 1:13-15 NIV [13]*When tempted, no one should say, "God is tempting me." For God cannot be tempted by evil, nor does he tempt anyone;* [14]*but each one is tempted when, by his own evil desire, he is dragged away and enticed.* [15]*Then, after desire has conceived, it gives birth to sin; and sin, when it is full-grown, gives birth to death.*

ANSWER | 1. Describe a time when God provided you a way out of a tempting situation?

2. Discuss the importance of the word "**when**" vs. **"if"** in James 1:13.

3. God does not tempt us. Why do you need to know this?

4. Where does temptation come from and where does it lead to when left unchecked?

5. Why do you think God allows us to be tempted... Are there any benefits?

Recognize

Start out by listing some common temptations that you may have encountered in the past or ones you expect to be faced with when living out your abstinence commitment.

1.

2.

3.

4.

5.

REFLECT | ## True Story - "One day you will crack"

Back in November, I went to a Silver Ring Thing Show, and it has changed my life completely. I've always been the shy "good girl". People are constantly telling me "One day you **WILL** crack", and you **WILL** have sex before marriage and do other stuff", or they say, "you **CAN"T** keep up this goody two-shoes act forever!"

After seeing the SRT show, something clicked, and I decided I had had enough of people telling me what I **CAN'T** do. Hearing the speakers gave me the courage to step out of my comfort zone and stand up for myself. I realized I have the power to do anything that I put my mind to, and I'm not alone out there.

I have always known that God is there to support me, but now I'm ready to prove all those boys wrong, and show them I can stay pure. Since the Silver Ring Thing event, I have become more confident, and I won't allow people to say those kinds of things to me.

I am my own person, and I can definitely stand up for what is right. Ever since I put my silver ring on, it has not left my finger, and it **WILL** stay there until marriage. Thanks for inspiring me to stay pure.

God Bless! Jenna

Key Scripture - "stand firm in the faith"

Once you have **recognized** temptation, you must make a conscience effort to **avoid** it. Scripture offers us this timely advice:

2 Timothy 2:22 NLT *[22]Run from anything that stimulates youthful lusts. Instead, pursue righteous living, faithfulness, love, and peace. Enjoy the companionship of those who call on the Lord with pure hearts.*

1 Peter 5:8-10 NIV *[8]Be self-controlled and alert. Your enemy the devil prowls around like a roaring lion looking for someone to devour. [9]Resist him, standing firm in the faith, because you know that your brothers throughout the world are undergoing the same kind of sufferings. [10]And the God of all grace, who called you to his eternal glory in Christ, after you have suffered a little while, will himself restore you and make you strong, firm and steadfast.*

Yeah, it's hard to do this…. But you're not alone! There are over 120,000 people and counting committed to abstinence who are wearing a SRT ring!

Hebrews 12:1-2 NLT [1] *Therefore, since we are surrounded by such a huge crowd of witnesses to the life of faith, let us strip off every weight that slows us down, <u>especially the sin that so easily trips us up.</u> And let us run with endurance the race God has set before us.* [2] *We do this by keeping our eyes on Jesus…*

You Can Do This…With God's Help! So What's Next?

LEARN

Avoid
Avoid situations that will lead you down the wrong road:
1. **Beware** of unplanned situations; Satan always has a plan for you.
2. **Beware** of doing stupid things before you do them
3. **Beware** of the company you keep
4. **Beware** of what you download
5. **Beware** of idle time, it's the devils workshop
6. **Beware** of being in the wrong places
7. **Beware** of the things that pull you down; Identify, avoid, and eliminate them
8. **Beware** of what you wear; "Don't advertise what you're not selling"
9. **Beware** of flirting; Don't be a tease
10. **Beware** of starting a relationship with people who only "appear" to share your values

ANSWER | **Your Thoughts**
Using the list from the previous page, identify 3 **"Bewares"** that would most likely cause you to fall into temptation and write the corresponding number in the blanks below. After identifying your areas of weakness, write a one sentence strategy for how you plan to avoid these pitfalls in the future.

Beware # ____

Beware # ____

Beware # ____

REFLECT | **Key Scripture - "Capture rebellious thoughts"**

2 Corinthians 10:5 NLT [5] *We destroy every proud obstacle that keeps people from knowing God. We capture their rebellious thoughts and teach them to obey Christ.*

Take evil thoughts captive:
When an evil thought comes into your mind, you must first recognize it, and then stop it cold, by requiring it to be submitted to Jesus Christ. You have a very short window to make the decision not to sin with regard to that thought. After that point, you're much less likely to stop resisting and give into temptation.

ANSWER | **Your Thoughts:**
When we think about sexual sin, more often than not we focus on the physical side of things. However, many times it's the **memories** of poor choices we've made that continue to haunt us long after the fact.

1. **Be Honest:** Are you struggling with some past sexual memories in your daily thought life?
   Yes   No

2. If so, what steps can you take to erase these memories from your mind?

LEARN | Minimize

Here are some strategies to consider, in order to minimize the effects of temptation. Depend upon God's power and not your own strength. In doing so, you will not allow the temptation to establish a firm foothold in your life. Consider this...Two thoughts can not occupy the mind at the same time. Change the thought that is tempting you, even if it means doing something silly like singing, "*Row, Row, Row Your Boat...*" to replace the thought. Try it, it actually works!

In Addition:

Don't rely on your own thinking, know God's word; Satan does not argue with scripture, he walks away

Don't take your relationship with the Lord for granted; Be in the word, and be in prayer

Don't try to be a hero; Enlist friends who can help you when you're struggling

Don't buy the lie that you're the only one struggling; Meet with your accountability partner

Don't allow your emotions to dictate your actions; Use your brain

Summary

Beware of the "Bird of Temptation"

When the "bird of temptation" lands on your head, you have two choices. You can "shoo" it away immediately, or you can allow it to linger for a while. If you allow the "bird of temptation" to linger, eventually it will build a nest. If you don't remove the nest, the bird will lay eggs that will soon give birth to more "birds of temptation." Eventually, you will have a full scale family of temptation on your head, raising havoc and dropping all kinds of garbage in your face. Before you know it, you're in "over your head" so to speak. If you're not alert, these temptations will come back year after year to roost, making it extremely difficult to free yourself from the resulting sin, once it has established its nest in your life.

Commit to the Plan:

1. **Recognize** temptation immediately and understand who is tempting you.

2. **Avoid** temptation by being aware of situations that will lead you down the wrong road.

3. **Minimize** the effects of any temptation that causes you to stumble by depending on God's power and not on your own strength.

Quote Scripture to the "bird of temptation" when it lands on your head, and it will fly away!

So, if purity and abstinence are the goal, and we assume that teenagers will eventually date, then it becomes essential to discuss boundaries before entering into any dating relationship with the opposite sex.

ANSWER | **Your Thoughts:**

1. Why do you think teenagers and young adults would rather "poke their eye out" than discuss "boundaries" with one another when entering into a relationship?

2. How would you bring up the "boundaries" subject with a person you have feelings for. What might you say?

3. What are some "red flags" you should be listening for when having this discussion?

LEARN | **The Battle for Our Hearts and Minds**

Protecting your sexual integrity is not just about **drawing a line in the sand** or about which behaviors are acceptable or not. It's more about the all out battle for our hearts and minds, as well as our bodies.

Use the following exercise to help understand that where you draw **"your line"** may be very different from others. Take a few minutes and list 5 actions in the appropriate box that you might do privately or in a relationship that you think are "too far" and 5 actions that you think are not "too far."

Use the following list for ideas… (Putting your arm around your BF or GF, dressing in a sexual manner, "going all the way," holding hands, hugging, spending a lot of time alone, oral sex, late night time together, viewing pornography, laying down together, light kissing, lingering kissing, passionate kissing, touching areas the "bathing suit covers", sexual dancing, etc. - Don't forget to include some from your own list).

ANSWER

<u>Definitely Too Far</u>
1.
2.
3.
4.
5.

<u>Not Too Far</u>
1.
2.
3.
4.
5.

Did you find it hard to list your answers?   Yes   No

If you answered "Yes"… why was it so difficult?

LEARN

Here's the Point:

The difficulty most of us find in arriving at a consistent answer from the lists on the previous page is exactly why this question is only answered in a vague way or not at all. But, make no mistake about it, this question **needs to be answered** and **clear boundaries** need to be established.

Start with this basic rule: "Don't touch what you don't have"... This will keep you out of a lot of trouble.

REFLECT

True Story - "I will never let anything like that happen again."

Hey Denny, I've noticed one major change in my life since I began wearing my silver ring. I have become more confident when dealing with a guy **I have gone a little too far with**. Every once in a while when my parents are not home, this guy and I will get together and sometimes get too close. We do some things we should not be doing. Whenever it happens I don't think about what is actually happening at the time. It takes a day or so for it to hit me. Then I say to myself, "I will never let anything like that happen again." But every time, I forget the promise I made and the same thing happens - but only worse and we go further than the last time. And when I try to talk to this guy about what we "did" together, he acts like nothing actually happened. I feel almost as if I am being used. The biggest problem is my parents and his parents are going out together in about a week. I think they are getting together to talk about us and their concerns about what we are doing together. I'm not sure what to do. I would really appreciate any advice you could give me. Thanks, Susan

ANSWER

Your Thoughts

1. What advice would **you** give to Susan?

| **Key Scripture - "Stay away from all sexual sin".**

1 Thessalonians 4:3-5; 7-8 NLT [3] *God's will is for you to be holy,* [4] *Then each of you will control his own body and live in holiness and honor -* [5] *not in lustful passion like the pagans who do not know God and his ways.* [7]*God has called us to live holy lives, not impure lives.* [8]*Therefore, anyone who refuses to live by these rules is not disobeying human teaching but is rejecting God, who gives his Holy Spirit to you.*

ANSWER

1. How does this scripture help to establish boundaries in determining "how far is too far?"

2. In your own words, describe what it means to control your body in a way that is holy and honorable to God.

3. How does having God's Holy Spirit affect your standards for establishing boundaries? (vs. 8)

LEARN | ## The Sense of Touch

"Touch is stronger than verbal or emotional contact. It can produce the most sensuous pleasure and set off our deepest emotions," according to Diane Ackerman in an excerpt from her book, *A Natural History of the Senses*, from Parade magazine 3/25/1990, pg.5.

She also quotes other experts who agree like Dr. Saul Schanberg, a professor at Duke University who says, "Touch is far more essential than our other senses. It affects (nearly) everything we do. No other sense can arouse you like touch." He concludes by saying, "We always knew that, but we never realized that it was biologically driven. If we didn't like the feeling of touching and patting each other, we wouldn't have sex."

Another expert, Dr. Tiffany Field, Ph.D. University of Miami Medical School states, "Touch affects the whole organism, as well as its culture and the individuals with whom it comes in contact. It's stronger than verbal or emotional contact."

ANSWER

Your Thoughts

1. God created the sense of touch... Why is that a good thing?

2. Touch can create such an explosion within us that is by far more impacting than our other senses. How can this quickly lead a person to lose control of their emotions?

3. If the person you're in a relationship with becomes a bit too "touchy, how should you respond?"

REFLECT

Key Scripture - "Honor God with your body"

1 Corinthians 6:18-20 NIV [18]*Flee from sexual immorality. All other sins a man commits are outside his body, but he who sins sexually sins against his own body.* [19]*Do you not know that your body is a temple of the Holy Spirit, who is in you, whom you have received from God? You are not your own;* [20]*you were bought at a price. Therefore honor God with your body.*

ANSWER

1. Define sexual immorality and explain why the Bible says it is like no other sin?

2. We are commanded to "flee from sexual sin." How do you plan to do that?

3. God says we are to honor him with our bodies. How will God let you know when you've gone too far physically?

Summary

Developing Non-Negotiable Boundaries

With all of this in mind, take 10 minutes and consider the concept of "waiting." Discuss how being "sexually-active" is a condition that starts in the mind, moves on to the sense of touch, works it's way down to the heart and soul (feelings) and leads many teenagers into acting out sexually.

Your Thoughts

1. Determine "how far is too far" and establish where **you will** draw the line regarding your physical limits.

2. In one or two sentences, describe how you plan to protect the emotional and spiritual aspects of your sexual purity.

LEARN	## Consequences

Pregnancy (In the U.S.A)
Neither condoms nor birth control pills are 100% effective in preventing pregnancy. So, the more times you have sex, the greater the risk you run of getting pregnant (or getting someone pregnant).

- Each year, 1 in 10 girls under the age of 20 (1 million per year) will become pregnant (2)
- 40% of these pregnancies will end in abortion (2)
- Nearly 1/3 of all girls will get pregnant as teenagers (3)

Sexually Transmitted Diseases (In the U.S.A.)
Condoms reduce the risk but do **NOT** eliminate the risk of acquiring STDs. So even if you use a condom correctly every time, you're **still at risk.**

- Each year, there are approximately 19 million new STD infections (4)
- 5% of girls and 30% of boys have sex by age 15 (5)
- 21% of teens in 9th grade have slept with **4** or more partners (5)
- 60% of sexually experienced teens say they wish they had waited longer to have sex (1)
- Teenagers who are sexually active are more likely to be depressed and attempt suicide (7)

REFLECT

Key Scripture - "Recognizing Sin in our Lives"

Matthew 5: 27 – 28 NLT [27] "You have heard the commandment that says, 'You must not commit adultery.' [28] But I say, anyone who even looks at a woman with lust has already committed adultery with her in his heart."

ANSWER

1. What do you think Jesus is trying to teach us concerning "hidden" sin?

2. How can sinning in your heart affect your ability to grow spiritually?

3. Why is your thought life as important to God as your outward actions?

LEARN

So What's it All Mean?

Sometimes sin can be very subtle and other times it can be very blatant. Just because you haven't gone "all the way" or "nearly all the way" doesn't mean you don't need to **start over**. Even if you've only let your thought life get out of control, you still need to get right with God. If you don't, you will find yourself in a spiritual battle, the likes of which you have never seen before.

- 77% of teens believe that "going all the way" is the only thing that constitutes sex and other sexual activities don't count (6)
- Statistics show that about 40% of teens who go online visit x-rated sites that show explicit content, either accidentally coming across the sites or being led to those sites (7)

REFLECT

True Story – "Counting the Emotional Costs"

Our daughter has been raised in a home where we talk about the importance of abstinence. She made an abstinence pledge as an eighth grader. She is now a junior and got mixed up with a guy who was not good for her. She had sex with him, and now we just found out that she has herpes. This news has been devastating to her and to us. My question is what can my husband and I do to help her and to help ourselves understand the emotional side of this? How can she forgive herself and know that God forgives her as well? We need your help.

Your Thoughts

1. What advice would you give these parents?

2. What would you say to your best friend if they shared this same story with you?

3. What does God say about forgiveness in his word?

Key Scripture - "Let the one who has never sinned throw the first stone!"

John 8:3-11 NLT [3] *As he was speaking, the teachers of religious law and the Pharisees brought a woman who had been caught in the act of adultery. They put her in front of the crowd.* [4] *"Teacher," they said to Jesus, "this woman was caught in the act of adultery.* [5] *The law of Moses says to stone her. What do you say?"* [6] *They were trying to trap him into saying something they could use against him, but Jesus stooped down and wrote in the dust with his finger.* [7] *They kept demanding an answer, so he stood up again and said, "All right, but let the one who has never sinned throw the first stone!"* [8] *Then he stooped down again and wrote in the dust.* [9] *When the accusers heard this, they slipped away one by one, beginning with the oldest, until only Jesus was left in the middle of the crowd with the woman.* [10] *Then Jesus stood up again and said to the woman, "Where are your accusers? Didn't even one of them condemn you?"* [11] *"No, Lord," she said. And Jesus said, "Neither do I. Go and sin no more."*

ANSWER | **Your Thoughts**
1. Was this really a life or death issue for this woman? Discuss your answer.

2. Why do you think Jesus forgave this woman even though she broke one of the 10 Commandments?

3. What do we learn about Jesus from this story?

LEARN | **True Repentance**
True repentance is a result of God's conviction and is more than just being **"sorry."** It's seeing that what you did was wrong, not just risky! It's turning around in God's strength and moving in a new direction... God's direction. It's the Holy Spirit getting your attention from within to convict you to stop what you've been doing wrong and to do a 180!

Stop for a second... Take a deep breath... Here's the Question...
Are you feeling **convicted** right now about a difficult sexual sin that's been haunting you for a while? Maybe you need to stop hiding it. Even before you get "**caught**", God wants to free you from this struggle!

Not only does God promise to forgive us when we ask, he also forgets. When a **Christian** asks for forgiveness and repents, God looks to your heart, he sees His Holy Spirit and it's as if you never sinned. Scripture tells us that "he has removed our sins as far as the east is from the west" (Ps.103:12). What an amazing gift that is to us.

The Importance of Forgiving Yourself

When we fall into sexual sin...many times we are our own worst enemies. This is especially true if we have grown up in a Christian home or attend youth group regularly. For some reason, sexual sin seems to be the one area we struggle with most, when it comes to forgiving ourselves.

REFLECT

Key Scripture - "he who sins sexually sins against his own body"

1 Corinthians 6:18-20 NIV *[18]Flee from sexual immorality. All other sins a man commits are outside his body, but he who sins sexually sins against his own body. [19]Do you not know that your body is a temple of the Holy Spirit, who is in you, whom you have received from God? You are not your own; [20]you were bought at a price. Therefore honor God with your body.*

ANSWER

1. Why is sexual sin such a "big" sin for Christians in particular...Why is no other sin like it?

2. Describe what you think a person feels like inside who attends youth group and church every week yet continues to live a sexually immoral life.

3. Explain what your life would look like if you didn't pay attention to this command from scripture, *"Flee from sexual immorality."*

LEARN | ## Forgive and Forget

Even though God's promise to forgive us is clear, we allow our guilt and shame to prevent us from finding true healing. Perhaps this is because only God has the ability to truly forgive and forget. When we sin sexually, it creates a memory that is not easily erased. And one of Satan's greatest weapons is to constantly remind us of our failures by bringing these memories to mind.

Take Action...Repent

Take a piece of paper and write down one or two things you seriously need God to forgive you for (especially any sexual sin you are feeling convicted of). When everyone is finished with this exercise, personally say a heartfelt prayer to the Lord and ask for His forgiveness. Next, destroy the paper, and ask your leader to dispose of it. Now...Make the decision to **"Let It Go!"**

Summary

So how do I start over? Remember to... T.R.U.S.T. God

Tell God specifically what you have done; Ask Him to forgive you for your sins and to give you the strength to start over.

Remove yourself from tempting situations that will cause you to slide back into bad behaviors. Often times this involves reevaluating the kinds of people you hang out with and putting specific boundaries in place.

Usually teenagers are unaware that they have been infected with an STD. Why... because up to 80% of those infected will show no symptoms for some STDs until later in life. Plan to get tested if you have been sexually active, in order to avoid experiencing irreversible damage from STDs.

An hour later, the officer returned and said, "I'm sorry, Ma'am. This has been a big mistake. When I pulled up behind you, I noticed your 'What Would Jesus Do?' license plate holder and your 'Follow Me to Sunday School' bumper sticker. I assumed the car was stolen!" (Our Daily Bread, 1 April 2008)

This is a funny story, but it is also a great illustration of those who commit to wear a silver ring, yet fail to fully give God control...They are vulnerable to ridicule because they're in the drivers seat, not God. When you compromise your abstinence commitment, even in small ways, that chink in your armor may be all it takes for Satan to attack. Satan is not worried if you're a Christian, as long as you don't act like one! If he can get you to live by the world's standards, he can damage your reputation, discredit your message, and dishonor the name of Christ in the process – often shaming you into walking away from your commitment altogether.

Bumper Stickers

Don't be faked out by trying to live out your Commitment, while operating outside of the power of the Holy Spirit. Create several "abstinence bumper stickers" that you would be embarrassed to have displayed on your car, if you were acting inappropriately. **Have a little fun with this**!

REFLECT | **Key Scripture – "Apart from me you can do nothing"**

John 15:5-8 NIV [5]*"I am the vine; you are the branches. If a man remains in me and I in him, he will bear much fruit; apart from me you can do nothing.* [6]*If anyone does not remain in me, he is like a branch that is thrown away and withers; such branches are picked up, thrown into the fire and burned.* [7]*If you remain in me and my words remain in you, ask whatever you wish, and it will be given you.* [8]*This is to my Father's glory, that you bear much fruit, showing yourselves to be my disciples.*

ANSWER

1. Discuss how a person becomes part of the vine.

2. How does being "attached to the vine" allow God to be in **full control** of your life?

3. Discuss what Jesus meant when he said, "*anyone who does not remain in me is like a branch that is thrown away and withers.*"

4. Apply this scripture to your abstinence decision - What promise does God give to those who "*remain in [Him]*" and keep their commitment until marriage?

REFLECT

True Story – "I discovered what was missing in my life…God."

In January, I attended a Silver Ring Thing Event and discovered what was missing in my life - God. Ever since then, I've been really good. Partying is no longer a thing that I look forward to on Friday nights or any nights for that matter. But I've struggled with the feeling of not being worth anything to a good Christian girl that hasn't made the same mistakes that I have. Trust me; I have really messed up in the past. After attending SRT, I realized that God has **COMPLETELY** restored me in *every* area of my life. That in His eyes I am made **new**. I've decided to give "wanting" a relationship with a girl a rest for a while. I've found that when I try to do things my way, they never last, and they always end in a "big" breakup. Instead I've let go and asked God to **take control**. After all, He only wants the best things for me - and that there's someone who will see me and accept me unconditionally. His name is Jesus - and He is more than enough. Thanks for staying in touch, **Jared**

LEARN

Supernatural Help

There is supernatural help available to overcome our natural instincts (hormones). God created us to be sexual beings, and he designed sex to be the thing that bonds married people together. It's when we take sex outside of marriage that we run into all kinds of trouble. When you are tempted, your natural sex drive gets kicked into overdrive. So, if you have any hope of surviving the years of sexual temptation, you will need **supernatural strength** to do it. This strength will not come from friends, parents, church, the media, a vow you make, or your silver ring on your finger. This power must come from inside, from the Holy Spirit operating within you and speaking to you in the moment of your greatest need. Don't settle for or depend on your natural strength. Instead, choose every day to develop your relationship with your **supernatural source**, the Holy Spirit, through prayer and spending time in God's word.

ANSWER	## Your Thoughts – How does supernatural strength (the Holy Spirit) work?

1. **It interrupts:** Ok, you're on the couch with your BF or GF, the lights are out, and your natural sexual instincts (hormones) are kicked in. Explain how the Lord has the **ability** to get your attention even when God is the furthest thing from your mind?

2. **It stops:** How does this source of "supernatural strength" stop you from acting on your natural sexual desires?

3. **It convicts:** How does this inner source convict you to change when you're "starting" to give in to sin?

4. **It wins:** Describe why it's essential to rely on the Holy Spirit's strength and not your own when battling all the prevailing forces that comes from sexual temptation.

LEARN	## Summary

Discuss: Make Sure You Know Why You are Waiting

1. God said it is the right thing to do
2. He called you to be set apart (1Thes. 4:3-4)
3. He created sex with a purpose
4. You can only give your virginity to one person
5. There are many blessings promised by God
6. No worrying about long-term consequences

Discuss: Make Sure You Understand the Struggle

1. There will be times when you won't care what God says, you'll want to follow your sexual appetite
2. It's more than choosing not to have premarital sex; It's about weighing the spiritual and emotional ramifications.
3. You will constantly be battling the mainstream media, peer pressure and other cultural influences.
4. You'll constantly hear that "it's impossible to wait"
5. You'll be told that you're the only one waiting

Discuss: Make Sure You Know How to Win the Battle

1. Don't rely on your own strength
2. Listen for the inner voice and respond
3. Never give up; If you fall short, ask for and receive God's forgiveness
4. Give God **complete control;** Remember that **supernatural strength** is available to you

REFLECT

Is God in complete control? He has a plan for your life.

Jeremiah 29:11-20 NIV *[11] For I know the plans I have for you," declares the LORD, "plans to prosper you and not to harm you, plans to give you hope and a future. [12] Then you will call upon me and come and pray to me, and I will listen to you. [13] You will seek me and find me when you seek me with all your heart.*

Settle the Control Issue Now

Righteous living is a matter of the will not of will power. The issue is will we surrender to the spirits leadership in our lives? (*Choosing to Wait: A Guide to Inspiring Abstinence;* Laura B. Gallier)

Below is a Suggested Prayer.

But before you even think about praying, consider this... You'll be asking God to do some major rearranging in your life. Guaranteed, some of it will not be easy or painless. You may have to walk away from some relationships or friends you've established over the years. But here in lies the control and trust issue. The question is...Will it be my way or God's way? There is only one right answer to this question and that's why this prayer is so important.

PRAY Dear God, I have come to the conclusion that I need you to be in control of my life. You know what's best for me. So I'm asking you to forgive me for all of my sins, for which I am so ashamed. Create in me a clean heart, O God; and renew a right spirit within me. I am sincere about my desire to be more like you, and I admit that I can't do it in my own strength. You have my permission to mold my character into your likeness. I'm asking you .to come into my life Lord. Please send your Holy Spirit to help shape my decisions and guide my actions. Help me to have the courage to live out my faith with conviction in **all** my relationships. Thank you Lord for hearing my prayer and answering it. I pray this all in your name Lord, Amen.

Now It's Time to Share Your Story and Make a Difference It's Time to... "Get It On"

next

DEVOTIONAL NOTE

References to *First Steps*, *Cornerstones*, or *Off and Running* are additional insights for students who have a copy of the Silver Ring Thing New Testament.

If you do not have a Silver Ring Thing New Testament feel free to skip this part of the devotional.

N E X T
Daily Devotions and Journal
by Denny Pattyn with Ashley Zahorian

Congratulations on making a commitment to spend time with God everyday. The decision you have made to "wait" is critical and life changing. Keeping your decision will be much more challenging! This devotional was created to help you stay strong in your commitment and to grow in your relationship with the Lord. Over 28 days, you will be led into a deeper personal relationship with almighty God. Don't take your relationship with Him for granted.

This 28-day devotional and journal is intended to be the **NEXT** step for those who have completed the 4 studies in the front of this book. Follow-up is critical if you want to get to the next level in your decision to wait. That being said, I hope to stay in touch with you along the way. Once a week, send an email to **devotions@silverringthing.com** (you will see weekly reminders). When you see the reminders, email me (Denny Pattyn) with your thoughts and tell me how God is working in your life. I want to hear back from you.

This devotional and journal will:
- Give you a reading plan to strengthen your relationship with Christ
- Help you reflect on Scripture daily
- Lead you through life issues and help you to write out your thoughts
- Inspire you to pray personally to God after every session
- Enable you to share devotions with your parents

One more thought:
Ask your parents if they would be interested in spending some time with you and with the Lord reading through these devotions together. You will be pleasantly surprised how much better your relationship with them will become simply by spending this time together. Try it!

1: Keeping Accountable   Today's Date: _____

Paul confronted Peter and Barnabas when they were not following the gospel.

When I saw that they were not following the truth of the Good News, I said to Peter in front of all the others, "Since you, a Jew by birth, have discarded the Jewish laws and are living like a Gentile, why are you trying to make these Gentiles obey the Jewish laws you abandoned? You and I are Jews by birth, not 'sinners' like the Gentiles. And yet we Jewish Christians know that we become right with God, not by doing what the law commands, but by faith in Jesus Christ. So we have believed in Christ Jesus, that we might be accepted by God because of our faith in Christ – and not because we have obeyed the law. For no one will ever be saved by obeying the law."

Galatians 2:14-16 NLT

If you made your abstinence pledge with SRT, you should have made your commitment with an accountability partner. This is a vital step in maintaining your pledge! Even Peter, one of the most important leaders of the early church, needed someone to keep him accountable. You and your accountability partner shouldn't just blindly support each other and assume the other is keeping his/her pledge.

Keep asking your accountability partner questions! Don't let each other justify impure behavior. Confronting someone you care about is never easy. Sometimes it might seem easier just to keep your mouth shut, but that's not "real love."

If you let borderline behaviors slide, you're giving the impression that you actually approve of what's going on. If you do that, you aren't being an accountability partner. Be a true friend, and help your friends strengthen their walk with God instead of letting them push God away.

Do you have an accountability partner? If so, what kind of relationship do you have with him or her?

Have you ever known that someone was right when he or she called you out on something? How did you react?

How do you share the truth with a friend who is making bad choices?

True friends tell the truth to one another
Say whatever you say in love
Remember to accept the truth from the Lord as well (Heb. 12:6)

2: God's Spotlight on Sin   Today's Date: _____

As a child of Christ, you are now in the light of the Lord.

For at one time you were darkness, but now you are light in the Lord. Walk as children of light (for the fruit of light is found in all that is good and right and true), and try to discern what is pleasing to the Lord. Take no part in the unfruitful works of darkness, but instead expose them. For it is shameful even to speak of the things that they do in secret. But when anything is exposed by the light it becomes visible, for anything that becomes visible is light. Therefore it says, "Awake, O sleeper, and arise from the dead, and Christ will shine on you."

Ephesians 5: 8-14 ESV

Review "First Steps" on page 303 of your SRT New Testament and focus on Point 3.

The closer you draw to God, the more you are able to resist sin and the more able you are to be in the light. Think of God's light as a flashlight on sin, which makes sense out of the darkness and reveals how evil sin is. Sometimes when the choices in your life get really confusing, the only way to see the right path is through God's light.

Take staying sexually pure, for example. It's going to be a huge challenge for you to resist sexual sin without God's grace! And when you draw closer to God, through Bible study, prayer, Christian fellowship, etc., you will have more strength to resist temptation. This doesn't mean that temptation will disappear, but being closer to God will help you to think more like God, and therefore, stay more pure!

How does being close to God help you to stay away from sin?

What is one way that you can draw closer to God today?

Write a brief prayer to God about a temptation you're struggling with.

I am always thinking of the Lord;
And because he is so near,
I never need to stumble or fall.
Psalm: 61:8 NLT

3: Saying No to Temptation

Today's Date: _____

Christ resisted the temptation of the devil.

Then Jesus was led up by the Spirit into the wilderness to be tempted by the devil. And after fasting forty days and forty nights, he was hungry. And the tempter came and said to him, "If you are the Son of God, command these stones to become loaves of bread." But he answered, "It is written, 'Man shall not live by bread alone, but by every word that comes from the mouth of God.'"
Again, the devil took him to a very high mountain and showed him all the kingdoms of the world and their glory. And he said to him, "All these I will give you, if you fall down and worship me." Then Jesus said to him, "Be gone, Satan! For it is written, 'You shall worship the Lord your God and him only shall you serve.'" Then the devil left him, and behold, angels came and were ministering to him.

Mathew 4:1-4, 8-11 ESV

Review "First Steps" on page 303 of your SRT New Testament and focus on Point 2.

Maybe you know someone at school who is so cool – he/she is always at concerts and plays guitar in a band. But every weekend, your parents won't let you go out to shows with your friend. They know something you don't – that your friend is really into drugs, and there have been some assaults at the club where your friend's band plays. You've pretty much accepted the fact that you're never going to get to go. Then one weekend, a miracle happens and your parents decide to let you go out with your friend! The next weekend, aren't you going to use, "but you let me last weekend!" as an argument in your weekly request? Won't that make it much harder for your parents to say no?
Just as your parents find it hard to say no after they've given in once, it's even harder to say no to the temptations of sin. Once you give in, it makes it that much easier to commit a sin again. Giving in also puts up a neon sign advertising to the devil that you might let him in again. Take strength in knowing that Christ is on your side, and that he resisted sin!

Why does giving into temptation once make it easy to do again?

What is a temptation that you struggle with?

How can you better resist temptation?

Resist the devil, and he will flee from you.
James 4:7 NLT

43

4: Prayer: Between You and God   Today's Date: _____

Pray to talk to God, not to show off to other people.

"And when you pray, you must not be like the hypocrites. For they love to stand and pray in the synagogues and at the street corners, that they may be seen by others. Truly, I say to you, they have received their reward. But when you pray, go into your room and shut the door and pray to your Father who is in secret. And your Father who sees in secret will reward you.
"And when you pray, do not heap empty phrases as the Gentiles do, for they think that they will be heard for their many words. Do not be like them, for your Father knows what you need before you ask Him."

Mathew 6:5-8 ESV

Read "First Steps" on page 9 of your SRT New Testament.

Prayer isn't about showing off for people. It's about a relationship with Christ. When you pray, talk **with** God! If you had a friend who you really wanted to have a deep conversation with, how would you do it? Would you talk with him/her in the middle of a crowd, as loudly as you could so that everyone would know that you were talking?

Probably not. You would go somewhere quiet, where you could really focus on that conversation. You wouldn't repeat yourself over and over again, but you would say what was really on your mind and in your heart. And you would really listen to what the other person had to say.

That's exactly how you should pray to God. He wants to be the most important person in your life and the best friend that you'll ever have! If you want him to be your best friend too, then treat him that way and truly talk with him.

What is the purpose of prayer?

How do you talk to a friend who you really care about? Do you listen?

Write a brief prayer to God, telling him how you want to know him.

Lord, thank you for the gift of prayer!
Thank you for the ability to talk to you
And to know that you really do care.

44

5: Forgiveness is for Everyone   Today's Date: _____

Love not only your friends, but also your enemies.

"You have heard that it was said, 'You shall love your neighbor and hate your enemy.' But I say to you, Love your enemies and pray for those who persecute you, so that you may be sons of your Father who is in heaven. For he makes his sun rise on the evil and on the good, and sends rain on the just and on the unjust. For if you love those who love you, what reward do you have? Do not even the tax collectors do the same? And if you greet only your brothers, what more are you doing than others? Do not even the Gentiles do the same? You therefore must be perfect, as your heavenly Father is perfect."

Matthew 5:43-48 ESV

Review "Cornerstones" on page 10 of your SRT New Testament.

It's pretty easy to love people that you like. It's a whole lot harder to love someone who you don't particularly care for. But if God asks us to love our enemies, then he will provide the way to do so.

Maybe there is someone at school who always picks on you, and you'd rather see him/her get expelled from school than see him/her happy. How can you fulfill God's calling to love that person when all he/she does is make you insane? It's not going to happen overnight. You have to pray for your own heart to change, and then begin to pray for the well-being of your "enemy." It may seem impossible at first, but God has a way of changing our hearts. He does it through his Holy Spirit who lives inside of us. Be different from your friends by letting God show you how to love those who are difficult to love. In the end, you will be the one who is truly transformed.

What does it mean to love your enemies? Do you have to like them?

Why is it so important to love people who you don't like?

Write out a brief prayer asking God to bless someone you don't like.

And as they stoned him, Stephen prayed,
"Lord Jesus, receive my spirit."
And he fell to his knees, shouting,
"Lord, don't charge them with this sin!" And with that, he died.
Acts 7:59-60 NLT

6: Hey, That's Not Cool   Today's Date: _____

Help each other to recognize sin and be free from it.

Dear brothers and sisters, if another Christian is overcome by some sin, you who are godly should gently and humbly help that person back onto the right path. And be careful not to fall into the same temptation yourself. Share each other's troubles and problems, and in this way obey the law of Christ. If you think you are too important to help someone in need, you are only fooling yourself. You are really a nobody.

Galatians 6:1-3 NLT

Read "Off and Running" on pages 232-233 of your SRT New Testament and focus on Point 1.

If you see that your friend's car is dripping brake fluid, would you tell her? Or would you just let her drive off, only to discover the damage when her brakes don't work? Of course not, you'd never let her leave the driveway!

So why do we hesitate to tell friends when something is wrong spiritually? If you're a good Christian friend, it's your duty to tell your friend if something is wrong. If you say it in love, and not in a judgmental "I'm better than you are" way, it should mean something to your friend.

While your friend might not be completely open to hearing what you have to say, you have to remember that it's what you've been called to do as a Christian friend. Not every part of following Christ is going to be easy, but it's the right thing to do. And wouldn't you want a friend to help you with problems in your life?

Are you ever afraid to confront a friend about a sin in his/her life? Explain.

Why is it hard to point out problems in a friend's life?

Do your parents ever correct you? How do you receive that correction?

Wounds from a friend are better
than many kisses from an enemy.
Proverbs 27:6 NLT

7: Saying Thank You

Today's Date: _____

Remember to thank God for what he does for you.

On the way to Jerusalem he was passing along between Samaria and Galilee. And as he entered a village, he was met by ten lepers, who stood at a distance and lifted up their voices, saying, "Jesus, Master, have mercy on us." When he saw them he said to them, "Go and show yourselves to the priests." And as they went they were cleansed. Then one of them, when he saw that he was healed, turned back, praising God with a loud voice; and he fell on his face at Jesus' feet, giving him thanks. Now he was a Samaritan. Then Jesus answered, "Were not ten cleansed? Where are the other nine? Was no one found to return and give praise to God except this foreigner?" and he said to him, "Rise and go your way; your faith has made you well."

Luke 17:11-19 ESV

Review "First Steps" on page 251 of your SRT New Testament and focus on Point 3.

The lepers never asked Christ to heal them; they only asked for mercy. Christ could have answered their prayers by giving them something to eat or even saying a kind word. Instead, Christ chose to feed their spirits by freeing them from leprosy. Leprosy was considered an "unclean" disease, and since it was contagious, leapers were completely excluded and isolated from regular life. Jesus gave them back the gift of living in community, along with the opportunity to witness God's mercy to them and their grateful families. See how Christ touched so many more than just the ten lepers!

What is important about the leper who came back to Christ was his thanks for Christ's mercy. The other nine were healed, and then hit the road! My guess is that the last leper is probably the only one who truly accepted Christ and was healed spiritually. His faith saved him. As for the rest, though they may not have accepted Christ, they still witnessed his goodness and perhaps helped, unwittingly, to bring others to God. He works with whatever little we give him.

E-mail me, Denny, at <u>devotions@silverringthing.com</u> with 1Y-7 as the subject with your answers to these questions

What does it really mean to be thankful?

Did any of the verses, reflections, or questions remind you of something going on in your life? If so, what?

What thoughts do you have about what you have studied thus far?

8: Going Home to Heaven   Today's Date: _____

We know God the Father through Christ. He has prepared a place for his followers in heaven.

"There are many rooms in my Father's home, and I am going to prepare a place for you. If this were not so, I would tell you plainly. When everything is ready, I will come and get you, so that you will always be with me where I am. And you know where I am going and how to get there."

"No, we don't know, Lord," Thomas said. "We haven't any idea where you are going, so how can we know the way?"

Jesus told him, "I am the way, the truth, and the life. No one can come to the Father except through me. If you had known who I am, then you would have known who my Father is. From now on you know him and have seen him!"

John 14:2-6 NLT

Read "Cornerstones" on page 124 of your SRT New Testament.

What's easier to explain to someone – something you can't see, like love, or something visible, like a hug? It's hard, in fact it's impossible, to understand God the Father without the Son. We need Christ as a visible sign of God's love and as a teacher.

Because God loves us so much, he never wants us to be separated from him. Christ **will** lead us to the Father, and to our ultimate home in heaven. It is because of Christ's love and sacrifice that we are saved. All we have to do is receive and accept that love and follow him where he leads.

Do you ever have trouble "hearing" God? Why do you think this happens?

What have you been able to learn about God without Jesus?

How do you picture the gates of heaven? Do you think anyone will ask you questions when you get there?

I just want to live my life for You
To receive the faith I know is true
– Something Like Real

9: Who Do You Live For?   Today's Date: _____

Follow only the true gospel of Christ, seeking the approval of God, not man.

I am astonished that you are so quickly deserting him who called you in the grace of Christ and are turning to a different gospel – not that there is another one, but there are some who trouble you and want to distort the gospel of Christ. But even if we or an angel from heaven should preach to you a gospel contrary to the one we preached to you, let him be accursed. As we have said before, so now I say again: If anyone is preaching to you a gospel contrary to the one you have received, let him be accursed.

For am I now seeking the approval of man, or of God? Or am I trying to please man? If I were still trying to please man, I would not be a servant of Christ.

Galatians 1:6-10 ESV

Part of what is unique about Paul is his decisiveness. Paul had been a leader in the Jewish church and the biggest persecutor of Christianity. Christ totally turned Paul's world upside down. Once he knew that Christ was God, Paul did a complete turnaround and was transformed into one of the most important leaders of Christianity.

As a result of his miraculous conversion, Paul followed God's will and didn't worry about what anyone else besides God thought. That's how we can tell that he was a man of God. He preached the gospel and lived out his life for God.

There will be people in your life who try to lead you astray from the gospel. Some people will demand that you prove your love for them by doing things that are contrary to the gospel, like having sex outside of marriage. The simple fact is, if you live for the approval of people instead of God, you're not going to find real truth or happiness.

List some examples of teaching or popular opinion that is contrary to God's word.

How can you tell if someone's teaching or ideas are right or wrong?

Who do you look to for approval in your life? Why?

Create in me a clean heart, O God,
And renew a right spirit within me.
Psalm 51:10 ESV

10: God's Forgiveness

Today's Date: _____

Christ died for us while we were still ungodly.

For while we were still weak, at the right time Christ died for the ungodly. For one will scarcely die for a righteous person – though perhaps for a good person one would dare even to die – but God shows his love for us in that while we were still sinners, Christ died for us. Since, therefore, we have now been justified by his blood, much more shall we be saved by him from the wrath of God. For if while we were enemies we were reconciled to God by the death of his Son, much more, now that we are reconciled, shall we be saved by his life. More than that, we also rejoice in God through our Lord Jesus Christ, through whom we have now received reconciliation.

Romans 5:6-11 ESV

Read "Cornerstones" on page 10 of your SRT New Testament.

Imagine you had a day start out really badly – maybe you slept in, because you snuck out and stayed out late the night before, missed a test, lied about why you were late to school, and snapped at everyone. When you finally got home and realized you had been a jerk all day, you wonder how God can still love you.

God loved us before we even knew him! He proved how unconditional his love and forgiveness are by taking the "first step." Christ came for everyone – even the people who hung him on a cross to die. He offers you love and forgiveness, no matter what! No matter what you do, God will always forgive you! In other words, you can start over today. Do not hold back. Accept the unconditional forgiveness of Christ!

How do you picture God's forgiveness?

Describe a time when you've felt God's love even when you didn't deserve it.

Write a brief prayer to God, thanking him for his love and forgiveness.

Long ago the Lord said to Israel: "I have loved you, my people, with an everlasting love. With unfailing love I have drawn you to myself."
Jeremiah 31:3 NLT

11: Never-Ending Joy   Today's Date: _____

Treat each other with love and keep your language clean.

Finally, all of you, have unity of mind, sympathy, brotherly love, a tender heart, and a humble mind. Do not repay evil for evil or reviling for reviling, but on the contrary, bless, for to this you were called, that you may obtain a blessing. For "Whoever desires to love life and see good days, let him keep his tongue from evil and his lips from speaking deceit; let him turn away from evil and do good; let him seek peace and pursue it. For the eyes of the Lord are on the righteous, and his ears are open to their prayer. But the face of the Lord is against those who do evil."

1 Peter 3:8-12 ESV

Read "Off and Running" on pages 308-309 of your SRT New Testament.

Imagine that someone you love has been on a long trip. Maybe your dad is in the military and has been serving overseas. You get to talk to him on the phone and by e-mail, but it's not the same…and you haven't seen him in more than two years. Even though he's been away for so long, you know how much he loves you and you can't wait to see him again.

At last, you're at the airport, waiting to see your dad come off of the plane. As he rounds the corner with a smile on his face, he drops his bags to give you the biggest hug of your life. How happy would you be? As happy as you are to be reunited with your dad, you'll be even happier when you see God face-to-face for the first time in heaven.

God has blessed you with an incredible gift – an eternal life filled with true joy. With God, you've found the most lasting source of joy and love! When he scoops you into his arms and hugs you, you will know that nothing in this world can compare to the love of your Father.

When are you the happiest?

Do you ever search for joy in places other than Christ? Why or why not?

Why is it dangerous to search for happiness through physical sources, such as sex?

Thank you for the gift of joy!
Help me to open my heart
To let you completely in.

12: Who Do You Live For?   Today's Date: _____

God made us his children. People who believe in Christ will keep themselves pure in Christ's example.

See how very much our heavenly Father loves us, for he allows us to be called his children, and we really are! But the people who belong to this world don't know God, so they don't understand that we are his children. Yes, dear friends, we are already God's children, and we can't even imagine what we will be like when Christ returns. But we do know that when he comes we will be like him, for we will see him as he really is. And all who believe this will keep themselves pure, just as Christ is pure.

1 John 3:1-3 NLT

Review "Cornerstones" on page 230 of your SRT New Testament and focus on Point 4.

There are two ways to live – for this world, following what society tells you, or for eternal life, following what God tells you. God has an awesome plan for you! You are one of his children! If you chose to follow the world, all you're doing is cheating yourself out of how amazing life can be. That doesn't mean that living a God-driven life will be easy. There will probably be times in your life when all you'll want to do is forget that you ever knew God, times when you won't want to worry about consequences. God will always forgive you, right?

That type of thinking is a trap, and it's one of the reasons why it's so important to let the Holy Spirit lead you. The Holy Spirit is the window through which the light of Christ enters your heart. Yes, God forgives. But God is also just, which means that we must deal with the earthly consequences of our actions. Also, whenever you sin, you put up a barrier to God; he never pushes you away, but you can push God away. It's essential that you seek and follow God's opinion first! He not only cares the most for you, but also has the best plan!

Who do you put first in your life?

Do you feel like God is calling you something specifically?

What is your biggest dream? Does God fit in?

If we are living now by the Holy Spirit,
Let us follow the Holy Spirit's leading in every part of our lives.
Galatians 5:25 NLT

13: Trading with God   Today's Date: _____

Christ took our punishment.

But now God has shown us a different way of being right in his sight – not by obeying the law but by the way promised in the Scriptures long ago. We are made right in God's sight when we trust in Jesus Christ to take away our sins. And we all can be saved in this same way, no matter who we are or what we have done.

For all have sinned; all fall short of God's glorious standard. Yet now God in his gracious kindness declares us not guilty. He has done this though Christ Jesus, who has freed us by taking away our sins. For God sent Jesus to take the punishment for our sins and to satisfy God's anger against us. We are made right with God when we believe that Jesus shed his blood, sacrificing his life for us. God was being entirely fair and just when he did not punish those who sinned in former times.

Romans 3:21-25 NLT

Review "Cornerstones" on page 16 of your SRT New Testament and focus on Point 2.

If you wreck your parents' car, even if they forgive you, someone still has to pay for the car to be repaired or replaced. If your parents pay for the car, then they've fixed the damage out of their pockets. So even if you are forgiven for your sins, there is still a price to be paid – the question is, who will pay it?

The payment for mistakes is the consequences part of forgiveness. God takes care of the eternal consequences of your sins, but you have to take responsibility for the earthly consequences because your actions affect others. Restitution is the proof of your sorrow whether in heaven or on earth. Those who have no intention of making restitution fear the Lord's mercy and spurn his forgiveness because it's too much work. Those of sincere heart welcome God's plan for their life.

Before Christ, everyone had to pay for his/her own sins, so it was really important to "follow the rules." But even the best people still mess up. There is no way that we can possibly pay the price for all of our debts, so Christ offers us a trade – his grace for the price of our sins. Pretty amazing, huh?

What is a "yoke?" (Hint: page 16 of your SRT New Testament.)

Have you ever forgiven someone that hurt you, but still felt hurt?

Is there anything that Christ's grace doesn't cover? Why or why not?

"Take my yoke upon you...and you will find rest for your souls."
Mathew 11:29 ESV

14: Got Spirit?

Today's Date: _____

Set your priorities on spiritual over physical training.

Have nothing to do with irreverent, silly myths. Rather train yourself for godliness; for while bodily training is of some value, godliness is of value in every way, as it holds promise for the present life and also for the life to come. The saying is trustworthy and deserving of full acceptance. For to this end we toil and strive, because we have our hope set on the living God, who is the Savior of all people, especially of those who believe.

1 Timothy 4:7-10 ESV

Read "First Steps" on page 221 of your SRT New Testament and focus on Point 1.

Do you ever feel like you're too young to be really strong spiritually? Like you are not yet ready, and that being a spiritual leader should be left to people who are a little older than you are? Sometimes it might seem tempting to put off spiritual growth and focus on what you can see in the physical world. But take heart! God uses the young to do his work and grants them great strength!

The two people Paul talks about most are two young disciples, Timothy and Titus. Most of the apostles of Jesus were young people when they met Christ and left everything to follow him! You have just as much potential to be strong spiritually as they were! Don't neglect your spiritual life just because you are young. Go out and rock the world; God can use you to do great things! The question is: are you willing to put spiritual ahead of worldly priorities?

E-mail me, Denny, at <u>devotions@silverringthing.com</u> with 1Y-14 as the subject with your answers to these questions:

Do you ever feel like you're not old enough to be a spiritual leader? Why or why not?

Did any of the verses, reflections, or questions remind you of something going on in your life? If so, what?

What thoughts do you have about what you have studied since I last asked you to e-mail me?

54

15: Represent

As part of God's people, you are called to a higher life.

But you are not like that, for you are a chosen people. You are a kingdom of priests, God's holy nation, his very own possession. This is so you can show others the goodness of God, for he called you out of the darkness into his wonderful light.

"Once you were not a people; now you are the people of God. Once you received none of God's mercy; now you have received his mercy."

Dear brothers and sisters, you are foreigners and aliens here. So I warn you to keep away from evil desires because they fight against your very souls. Be careful how you live among your unbelieving neighbors. Even if they accuse you of doing wrong, they will see your honorable behavior, and they will believe and give honor to God when he comes to judge the world.

1 Peter 2:9-12 NLT

Read "Cornerstones" on page 310 of your SRT New Testament and focus on Point 1.

"Don't advertise what you aren't selling," is a Silver Ring Thing slogan which means that if you aren't looking for a sexual relationship, don't dress like you are. The slogan also means that you should not flirt, touch other people, or lead them to think that you are interested in a relationship that "may" involve sex.

This principle applies to every aspect of your life – if you act in a non-Christian way, people will get both a bad impression of you and of Christianity. Does that mean you will be perfect? Of course not! Everyone messes up. But it does mean – whether you like it or not – that people are watching you. Some people will watch the way you live your life waiting for you to make a mistake. Pray daily that God will protect you from falling into all the traps that the devil has set. This is a prayer he will be sure to answer!

What impression do people get when they look at you? Do they immediately think that you're a Christian?

How important are first impressions to you?

How can you see past what someone looks like to who he/she really is?

Lord, help me to be a light
And to live my Christian faith.

55

16: God Is Not Going Anywhere   Today's Date: _____

God will come through on his promises, and the Spirit is the guarantee.

Furthermore, because of Christ, we have received an inheritance from God, for he chose us from the beginning, and all things happen just as he decided long ago. God's purpose was that we who were the first to trust in Christ should praise our glorious God. And now you also have heard the truth, the Good News that God saves you. And when you believed in Christ, he identified you as his own by giving you the Holy Spirit, whom he promised long ago. The Spirit is God's guarantee that he will give us everything he promised and that he has purchased us to be his own people. This is just one more reason for us to praise our glorious God.

Ephesians 1:11-14 NLT

Review "First Steps" on page 221 of your SRT New Testament and focus on Point 3.

God could have just created us and then left us to fend for ourselves on earth. In fact, some people believe he did just that. But that wasn't his plan – he made us to love each other and him! He even programmed us to actively search for him and his love.

A few years ago, the cover story of *Newsweek Magazine* reported how human brains are actually hard wired to seek out a higher being! Why would we be wired for a God that didn't exist? What better proof of his existence could there be? And better yet, why would a God who didn't care about us design us to yearn for him?

When you decided to walk with Christ and heard the Good News that God was your true and loving father, you acknowledged your true identity. When you got serious about God, you formally accepted the gift that had always been intended for you. You officially became part of God's great family and plan for mankind! God – who goes to such lengths to ensure your happiness – will never abandon you no matter what you do or what happens to you. That is guaranteed through the Holy Spirit.

How do trials help you grow?

Describe a time when you may have doubted God; was the doubt well-founded?

Write a brief prayer to God thanking him for always caring about you.

This is why we never give up.
Though our bodies are dying, our spirits are being renewed every day.
2 Corinthians 4:16 NLT

17: Hope Does Not Disappoint Us   Today's Date: _____

Use trials and persecution as an opportunity to tell people why you hope.

Now, who will want to harm you if you are eager to do good? But even if you suffer for doing what is right, God will reward you for it. So don't be afraid and don't worry. Instead, you must worship Christ as Lord of your life. And if you are asked about your Christian hope, always be ready to explain it. But you must do this in a gentle and respectful way. Keep your conscience clear. Then if people speak evil against you, they will be ashamed when they see what a good life you live because you belong to Christ. Remember, it is better to suffer for doing good, if this is what God wants, than to suffer for doing wrong!

1 Peter 3:13-17 NLT

Review "First Steps" on page 221 of your SRT New Testament and focus on Point 4.

Events that God sends our way have meaning. When we look back on events in our lives through God's perspective, we can see they really did have meaning. We then wonder why we worried and why we were so hard on ourselves. We can also identify what clues and signposts God was posting in our path. But in the end, remember that God will specifically use each event to inform us of his will.

Events by themselves don't have meaning; we must invest them with meaning. Sometimes we're good at this and sometimes we're not. But prayer can help us discern God's intention. Think about it; if we can get some clues about where we're headed, we're usually pretty happy. Even when the meaning eludes us, we should accept God's intention for our lives and honestly do our best.

Life challenges our spirit, and we should also consider how God designed our experiences to amaze and dazzle us with the depth of his love and caring.

Next time something happens that you don't expect, try to figure out the message that God is sending your way. Maybe God is giving you a challenge so you can help someone else. Maybe God is preparing you for something really big. Either way, the choice is yours as to who you will trust...yourself or God. Think about it.

How has a trial in your life been a witnessing opportunity?

Have you ever lost hope in a big way? Explain.

Through suffering, these bodies of ours constantly share in the death of Jesus so that the life of Jesus may also be seen in our bodies.
2 Corinthians 4:10 NLT

18: Stand by Me

Real friends stand out from fake friends when the going get tough.

Don't just pretend that you love others. Really love them. Hate what is wrong. Stand on the side of the good. Love each other with genuine affection, and take delight in honoring each other.

When God's children are in need, be the one to help them out. And get into the habit of inviting guests home for dinner, or, if they need lodging, for the night.

When others are happy, be happy with them. If they are sad, share their sorrow.

Romans 12:9-10, 13, 15 ESV

Review "Off and Running" on pages 232-233 of your SRT New Testament and focus on Point 3.

Have you ever had a friend who only seems interested in your friendship when life is great? Or you may have a friend who only hangs out with you when you get into trouble. A good friend will be with you for the good and the bad – not one or the other!

Having good Christian friends – and being a good friend – isn't just something "cool." It's absolutely essential. So what does being a good friend mean?

Here are a few ideas on how to be a good friend, taken from the best guide there is – the Bible!

✓ Be excited when your friends succeed!
✓ Pray for, encourage, and help your friends, even if it won't benefit you.
✓ Be there for your friends when they mess up.
✓ Be a loving, warm friend especially when times are hard.
✓ Stand up for your friends when others don't.
✓ Take the high road and be faithful to your friends even when they push you away.

Did any of these points hit particularly close to home? Explain.

How do the above traits also apply to your relationship with your parents?

Which of the above friendship traits do you need to work on?

Lord, thank you for the gift of friendship!
Help me to be a real friend all the time.
Thank you for your eternal friendship in my life

Love is selfless, and will last forever.

Love is patient and kind; love does not envy or boast; it is not arrogant or rude. It does not insist on its own way; it is not irritable or resentful; it does not rejoice at wrongdoing, but rejoices with the truth. Love bears all things, believes all things, hopes all things, endures all things.
Love never ends. As for prophecies, they will pass away; as for tongues, they will cease; as for knowledge, it will pass away. For we know in part and we prophesy in part, but when the perfect comes, the partial will pass away.
1 Corinthians 13:4-9 ESV

Review "Off and Running" on page 204 of your SRT New Testament and focus on Point 2.

What do you really mean when you say, "I love you"? Love is a word that gets thrown around a lot. "I love you, you're my best friend ever!" "I love you, you're so hot!" "I love football!" and then the big ones, like "I love you, until death do us part."
Before you get into a relationship, think about why you're attracted to the other person. Is it physical? Is it because they're a good friend? Or is there something deeper?
If you try to base a relationship on physical attraction or just friendship, it's going to eventually fail. Don't forget that dating is a way to learn about marriage, and to discover what kind of person matches with you. Dating needs to be based on a much, much deeper kind of love – the love God shares with you!

What are the three Greek descriptions of love? (Hint: page 204 of your SRT New Testament.)

Do you think the word love is ever misused? Why or why not?

Why is it dangerous to get into a serious relationship if you aren't ready for it, or go into it for the wrong reasons? Explain.

Many waters cannot quench love,
neither can floods drown it.
Song of Solomon 7:4 ESV

20: Peace in Christ   Today's Date: _____

The Father is revealed through Christ, who gives peace.

"All things have been handed over to me by my Father, and no one knows the Son except the Father; and no one knows the Father except the Son and anyone to whom the Son chooses to reveal him. Come to me, all who labor and are heavy laden, and I will give you rest. Take my yoke upon you, and learn from me, for I am gentle and lowly in heart, and you will find rest for your souls. For my yoke is easy, and my burden is light."

Mathew 11:27-30 ESV

Read "Cornerstones" on page 16 of your SRT New Testament and focus on Point 1.

There are a lot of things in this world that offer temporary peace. A relationship, a movie, a sexual experience, or a night of drugs or alcohol can all offer promises of peace. But that peace won't last! The comfort of sex and substances will be especially short lived, and will usually leave you less happy than you were in the first place.

But Christ's peace is real, because well...he's God. God's love is ultimate and he will always love you, no matter what you do! Do you have that kind of security with anyone or anything else? Even the best human relationship can be lost or destroyed, and the feelings of peace that went with it. But God's love is unconditional, and even if you completely blew him off or tried to hurt him, he would still love you. In order to receive the peace that comes from that love, all you have to do is go to Christ!

Where can you find lasting peace?

In what ways in the past have you searched for peace?

Why is it important to receive Christ?

Lord, I'm ready to make you the center of my life.
Thank you for your love and peace
And for taking on the burden of my sins.

60

21: Getting Clean

Jesus Christ is our pleader before the Father, who takes the price for our sins. Belong to God by obeying him.

My dear children, I am writing this to you so that you will not sin. But if you do sin, there is someone to plead for you before the Father. He is Jesus Christ, the one who pleases God completely. He is the sacrifice for our sins. He takes away not only our sins but the sins of all the world.

And how can we be sure that we belong to him? By obeying his commandments. If someone says, "I belong to God," but doesn't obey God's commandments, that person is a liar and does not live in the truth. But those who obey God's word really do love him. That is the way to know whether or not we live in him. Those who say they live in God should live their lives as Christ did.

1 John 2:1-6 NLT

Review "First Steps" on page 303 of your SRT New Testament and focus on Point 4.

Say a little kid did something his parents told him not to, and then ran and asked for forgiveness. If his parents assured him he was forgiven, would he need to run back to them the next day asking for forgiveness for the same mistake? If he did that every day, wouldn't it be an insult to his parents, like the parents saying he was forgiven wasn't good enough?

When you ask God to forgive you for a sin, it is forgiven! End of story! So take comfort in accepting God's forgiveness, and letting go of the hold the sin had in your life! Once you accept God's forgiveness, run with it and break free from even the memory of the sin. Learn whatever lesson God has taught you through it, but use it as a chance to move on and make positive changes in your life. God not only forgives your sin, but Jesus paid the price for it through death on the cross! It's an awesome gift, treasure it.

E-mail me, Denny, at <u>devotions@silverringthing.com</u> with 1Y-21 as the subject with your answers to these questions:

How does accepting God's forgiveness help you to avoid other sin?

Did any of the verses, reflections, or questions remind you of something going on in your life? If so, what?

What thoughts do you have about what you have studied since I last asked you to e-mail me?

22: Asking for Help   Today's Date: _____

God will provide for you, just as he provided for Paul.

As you know, you Philippians were the only ones who gave me financial help when I brought you the Good News and then traveled on from Macedonia. No other church did this. Even when I was in Thessalonica you sent help more than once. I don't say this because I want a gift from you. What I want is for you to receive a well-earned reward because of your kindness.

At the moment I have all I need – more than I need! I am generously supplied with the gifts you sent me with Epaphroditus. They are a sweet-smelling sacrifice that is acceptable to God and pleases him. And this same God who takes care of me will supply all your needs from his glorious riches, which have been given to us in Christ Jesus.

Philippians 4:15-20 NLT

Review "First Steps" on page 251 of your SRT New Testament and focus on Point 2.

"All you had to do was ask." How often have you heard these words? How often do you say them? God already knows everything you need, but he wants you to ask him for help. When we ask for help, it shows that we need God and we give God control of our lives, so the good we accomplish ultimately gives glory to God.

Sometimes your parents wait until you ask before they help with a problem. If you need help making a car payment, they could make a direct deposit without even telling you, but would you really appreciate that? Parents wait to be asked because they know that having a child ask for help is more meaningful than simply giving help. Asking offers us the chance to acknowledge our dependence and to say "thank you." So admitting that you need help from God is part of reaching out, to God, in faith.

What is your reaction to a friend who refuses to ask for help?

How does it make you feel when someone asks you for help or advice?

Do you struggle with asking for help? Why or why not?

Lord, help me to put you first.
Thank you for always loving me,
Even when I forget to ask you for help.
I want to trust in your plan for my life.

Today's Date: _____

Treat each other with love and forgiveness.

Put on then, as God's chosen ones, holy and beloved, compassion, kindness, humility, meekness, and patience, bearing with one another and, if one has a complaint against another, forgiving each other; as the Lord has forgiven you, so you also must forgive. And above all these put on love, which binds everything together in perfect harmony. And let the peace of Christ rule in your hearts, to which indeed you were called in one body. And be thankful. Let the word of Christ dwell in you richly, teaching and admonishing one another in all wisdom, singing psalms and hymns and spiritual songs, with thankfulness in your hearts to God. And whatever you do, in word or deed, do everything in the name of the Lord Jesus, giving thanks to God the Father through him.

Colossians 3:12-17 ESV

Review "Cornerstones" on page 70 of your SRT New Testament and focus on Point 3.

When God forgives you for your sins, all you see is the end result of that forgiveness – your freedom from the sin. But the consequences of sin don't just magically disappear; instead, God takes them on himself and pays the consequences. That's why Christ had to die on the cross for us – in order to pay for the death we deserve.

If you forgive someone, it breaks the chain of the consequences of your friend's actions; it means that you take on the responsibility. When you chose to forgive out of love, there's always sacrifice involved. If a friend hurts you, you still have to deal with the pain when you forgive him/her.

Sometimes the consequences for our actions are more than any other human can take. Christ takes on the responsibility for the moral sin on our souls when we accept him. God will also help you to forgive others. When we love others, we'll be able to share part of the forgiveness that Christ has given us. But without love, we have nothing!

Describe an experience when someone forgave you and took on the responsibility for what you did.

How do you make up for what you've done wrong, while accepting the forgiveness of Christ?

Write out a brief prayer to Christ, thanking him for his sacrifice for you.

*"If you forgive those who sin against you,
Your heavenly Father will forgive you."*
Matthew 6:14 NLT

24: How Can You Tell What's Wrong?   Today's Date:_____

God sees everything that we think and do. Christ faced the same temptations as we do, but did not fall for them; God gives us grace.

Indeed, the word of God is living and effective, sharper than any two-edged sword, penetrating even between soul and spirit, joints and marrow, and able to discern reflections and thoughts of the heart. No creature is concealed from him, but everything is naked and exposed to the eyes of him to whom we must render an account.

Therefore, since we have a great high priest who has passed through the heavens, Jesus, the Son of God, let us hold fast to our confession. For we do not have a high priest who is unable to sympathize with our weaknesses, but one who has similarly been tested in every way, yet without sin. So let us confidently approach the throne of grace to receive mercy and to find grace for timely help.

Hebrews 4:12-16 NAB

Review "First Steps" on page 277 of your SRT New Testament and focus on Point 2.

Sometimes it seems like there are shortcuts in life. You can cheat on a test, get a good grade, and maybe never get caught. But you will have to live with knowing that you didn't earn the grade and don't even know the material. Your good grade could even hurt others in the class by skewing the grading curve. In the same way, if you can go too far with a girlfriend or boyfriend, you might be able to keep it a secret. But you will carry the memory and maybe even scars with you forever, and God will always know what you've been doing.

God knows everything we do, even our darkest secrets – and he still loves us! But when we do things that are wrong, it hurts us because we become a little less human, and step a little further away from what God wishes for us. That pushes us away from God. Use the word of God to discover what is wrong with your life. Then ask God for help! When it seems like staying pure is impossible, ask God for the same grace that enabled Jesus to stay pure and sinless. God will give you the same grace and determination that enabled Christ to face the cross. God will never ask you to do something that you can't do; he never tires of loving us, no matter how much we mess up!

What temptations do you struggle with?

How can you be more open with God about your life?

How can you use the Bible as the guide God intended it to be?

For if we are faithful to the end, trusting God as firmly as when we first believed, we will share in all that belongs to Christ.
Hebrews 3:14 NLT

Pray always! Pray for yourselves, and for each other.

Are any among you suffering? They should keep on praying about it. And those who have reason to be thankful should continually sing praises to the Lord. Are any among you sick? They should call for the elders of the church and have them pray over them, anointing them with oil in the name of the Lord. And their prayer offered in faith will heal the sick, and the Lord will make them well. And anyone who has committed sins will be forgiven.

Confess your sins to each other and pray for each other so that you may be healed. The earnest prayer of a righteous person has great power and wonderful results. Elijah was as human as we are, and yet when he prayed earnestly that no rain would fall, none fell for the next three and a half years! Then he prayed for rain, and down it poured. The grass turned green, and the crops began to grow again.

James 5:13-18 NLT

Review "First Steps" on page 251 of your SRT New Testament and focus on Point 4.

Have you ever prayed to God asking for something so big that you never really expected to get it? Maybe to get an "A" on a test you bombed, or for that "special" guy or girl to suddenly think you're the most interesting person in the world? Christ prayed to the Father that he might be spared from the cross. That's a pretty extreme prayer, but he asked in a spirit of thanks and acceptance of the Father's will. And he embraced the Father's plan – our salvation.

After you've stopped worrying and prayed thankfully for God's help, something really cool happens: peace! God's answer might not be what you want to hear, but you'll be cool about it because you'll know it's his will, and that he will take care of you!

What is the craziest thing you've ever asked Christ for?

Was the answer different from what you expected?

Write out a brief prayer really asking God for help with a problem you're experiencing, and thank him in advance for the solution!

Thank you Jesus! I trust in you.
Thank you for what I know you are going to do in my life!

What you say is powerful.

Not many of you should become teachers, my brothers, for you know that we who teach will be judged with greater strictness. For we all stumble in many ways, and if anyone does not stumble in what he says, he is a perfect man, able also to bridle his whole body. If we put bits into the mouths of horses so that they obey us, we guide their whole bodies as well. Look at the ships also: though they are so large and are driven by strong winds, they are guided by a very small rudder wherever the will of the pilot directs. So also the tongue is a small member, yet it boasts of great things.

How great a forest is set ablaze by such a small fire! And the tongue is a fire, a world of unrighteousness. The tongue is set among our members, staining the whole body, setting on fire the entire course of life, and set on fire by hell.

James 3:1-6 ESV

Review "Off and Running" on page 264 of your SRT New Testament and focus on Point 2.

Every year, fires devastate acres and acres of forests. How often do you hear about a fire being caused by a camper carelessly starting a fire and letting it get out of hand? Just as a spark can set woods ablaze, careless words can fuel verbal fires. Gossip spreads very quickly! But you can stop the fires from ever starting by not spreading hurtful rumors.

Be careful not to spread rumors. Even if you say something in "secret," chances are that half your school will have heard about it by the next day. The best first step in getting to the bottom of a rumor is talking to the person who it's about. Really listen to what that person has to say! Then you'll get to hear his/her side of the story, and talk with the person directly instead of getting all your facts secondhand.

How careful are you with what you say?

Describe a time when you've seen a rumor get out of control.

Have you ever been hurt by a rumor? Explain.

My dear brothers and sisters,
Be quick to listen, slow to speak, and slow to get angry.
James 1:19 NLT

Today's Date: _____

Children should obey their parents, and parents should nurture their children.

Children, obey your parents in the Lord, for this is right. "Honor your father and mother" (this is the first commandment with a promise), "that it may go well with you and that you may live long in the land." Fathers, do not provoke your children to anger, but bring them up in the discipline and instruction of the Lord.
Ephesians 6:1-4 ESV

Review "Off and Running" on pages 158-159 of your SRT New Testament and focus on Point 4.

Do you pray for your friends? What about your family? Praying for the people you care about (and even those you don't) is important because God listens to prayer! It might not be in the timing or in the way that you expect, but God will listen to your prayers.
I don't know what your relationship is like with your parents; every single relationship is different. Hopefully you have a relationship based on trust. No matter how close or distant you are from your parents, keep each other in prayer! Even if you don't understand why you have the family you do, remember that God has a reason for putting you all together.
Remember God never said, "Honor your father and mother if they are perfect." He expects you to honor them because you can trust a perfect God to make things, "go well with you." That is a promise you can count on, even when you are experiencing a major problem in your family. God is paying attention and will bless you if you trust him by honoring your parents.

How often do you pray for your family?

Do you "honor" your parents?

Write out a brief prayer for your family, especially for your parents.

"Honor your father and your mother,
That your days may be long in the land
The Lord your God is giving you."
Exodus 20:12 ESV

28: Christ Can Relate

Today's Date: _____

Jesus cried out and then died on the cross.

At noon, darkness fell across the whole land until three o'clock. Then, at that time Jesus called out with a loud voice, "Eloi, Eloi, lema sabachthani?" which means, "My God, my God, why have you forsaken me?"

Some of the bystanders misunderstood and thought he was calling for the prophet Elijah. One of them ran and filled a sponge with sour wine, holding it up to him on a stick so he could drink. "Leave him alone. Let's see whether Elijah will come and take him down!" he said.

Then Jesus uttered another loud cry and breathed his last. And the curtain in the Temple was torn in two, from top to bottom. When the Roman officer who stood facing him saw how he had died, he exclaimed, "Truly, this was the Son of God!"

Mark 15:33-39 NLT

Review "Cornerstones" on page 70 of your SRT New Testament and focus on Point 2.

Imagine the abandonment that Christ must have felt when he died on the cross. His friends had betrayed him; one of his most trusted apostles, Peter, denied his friendship with Christ not once, but three times; and the people who Jesus came to save had beaten him and hung him on a cross to die. Even though he knew the Father's plan, Christ still felt total abandonment on the cross and called out to God.

Have you ever experienced being left out? Maybe your friends decided to move in a different direction and not to include you in their new activities. It's incredibly painful to not be included. Jesus can empathize. He experienced everything that we do, and so much more, including being left out! Christ can bring you comfort and peace even when it feels like you don't have any real friends. He heals our hearts when we're broken and when we feel alone.

E-mail me, Denny, at <u>devotions@silverringthing.com</u> with 1Y-28 as the subject with your answers to these questions:
Describe a time when you've felt alone.

How can you connect with God when you feel abandoned by others?

What thoughts do you have about what you have studied through out this book? Share with me how you have been blessed and grown closer to God if that's been the case.